The Dark Palace

KW-327-204

95800000184354

Written by Zoë Clarke

Illustrated by Beatriz Castro

RISING STARS

Windsor and Maidenhead

Many people thought Gemma Prince's house was odd. It had a tall, central tower with a garden on the roof. Gigantic, flowering creepers exploded out of the chimney stack.
There were lots of secret doorways and deep, dark cellars. Gemma had breakfast in the tree house and dinner in the greenhouse.

The one thing Gemma didn't like about her house was how quiet it was. Her parents had very few friends, and she wished they could share it with more people.

Gemma walked through the city every day. There were interesting things to find there if you hunted in the right places. Her dad called them 'hidden gems'.

It was an icy morning when Gemma ran down a cobbled alleyway and found a pleasant courtyard. There was a statue of a dancer in the centre.

In the far corner of the courtyard, something caught Gemma's eye. Something interesting. Gemma realised she had found her own hidden gem.

The broken windows looked a bit sad, but when Gemma stared hard, she could make out some words over the door. In faded lettering, it said: The Dance Palace.

In her head, Gemma could hear soft music that
made her feel as light as a feather. Her feet
began to twitch, and she started to twirl around
the courtyard.

All too soon, Gemma had to go to her lessons,
but she made up dance steps all the way there.
Later on, in computer club, Gemma found
some old photographs of the city.

There was a Dance Street and a Dance Road ... and then, success! Gemma found some old black and white photographs of The Dance Palace. Once, it had been a venue for parties and fun!

In one old photograph, lots of people were queueing up outside. A fancy lady was wearing a long dress with sparkling gemstones, and feathers in her hair.

There was a newspaper report, too.

GIANT FIRE DESTROYS DANCE PALACE!

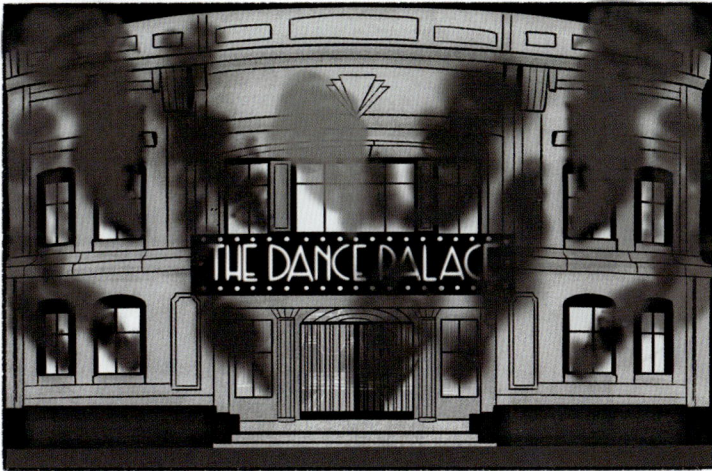

"The Dance Palace may have to shut for good," said Mr Lance, the owner.

Gemma's dance teacher was called Mr Lance. Could he tell her about the fire? Gemma went to speak to him after her lessons.

Mr Lance told Gemma that his grandfather had owned The Dance Palace before the fire. He had some old film reels and photographs from when it was open.

Old
Photographs

Mr Lance looked sad, so Gemma made a plan. She asked to borrow the photographs and the film, and then she called her friends for help.

Gemma's garden had tall brick walls. Gemma and her friends hung up giant, white sheets to use instead of a screen.

The old photographs were gently pinned to notice boards and Gemma put a New Dance Palace poster outside the greenhouse. They hung up lights and gemstones, which glinted like ice.

Soon, the garden was ready. Gemma made a card for Mr Lance.

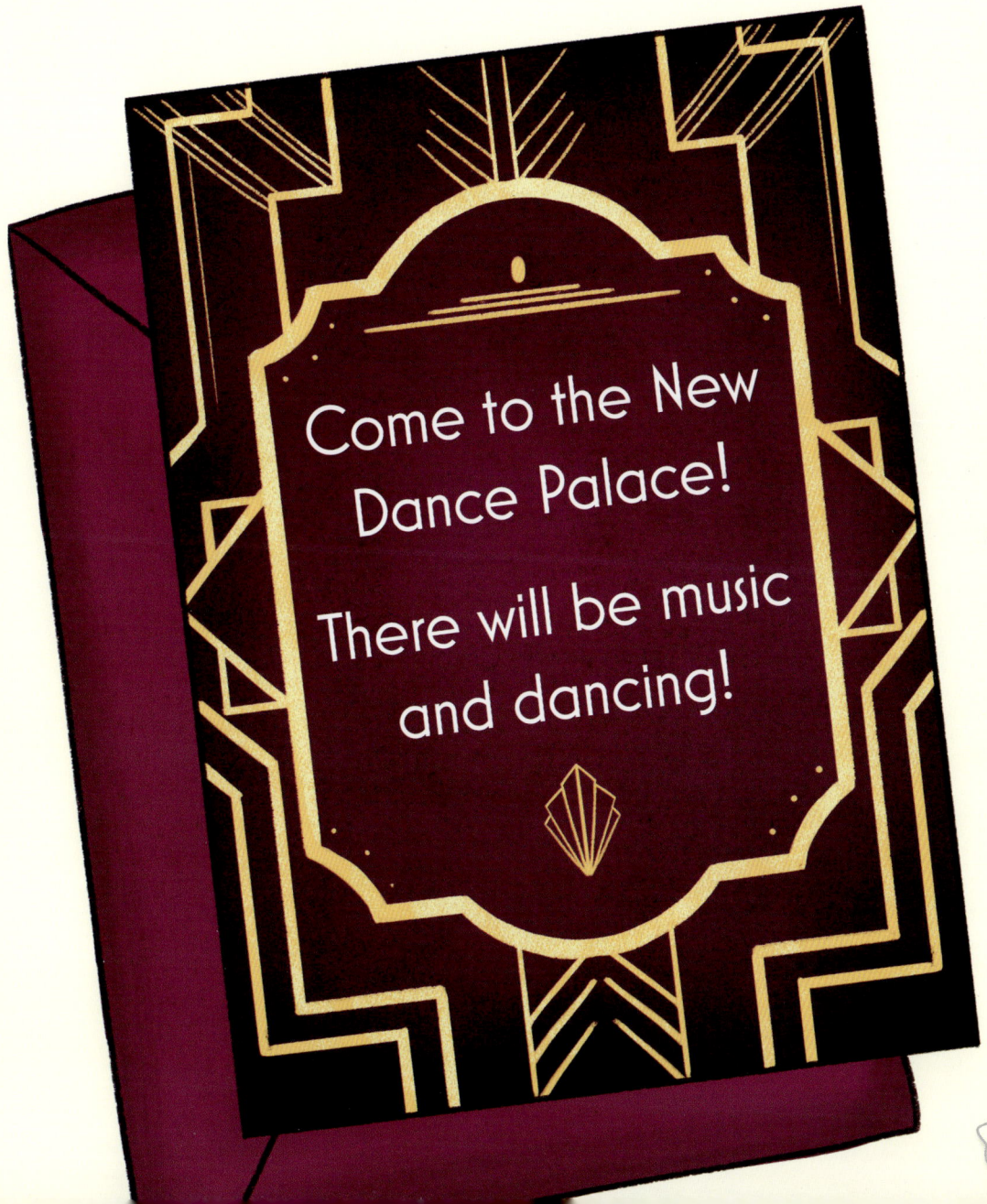

Come to the New Dance Palace!

There will be music and dancing!

Mr Lance was thrilled when he saw the photograph display. All of his dance students were there, and everyone enjoyed seeing his films of people dancing.

"You are a genius!" he told Gemma.

THE NEW DANCE PALACE

Then, Mrs Prince got her flute and Mr Prince got his violin. Their home was filled with music and dancing! Everyone twirled in the moonlight at the New Dance Palace.

Phonics Practice

Say the sound and read the words.

/s/	c (e, i, y)

December   city   cinema   icy   cyclone

/j/	g (e, i, y)

genius   gemstone   giraffe   gigantic   energy

/s/	-se

house   mouse   horse   nurse   purse

/s/	-ce

prince   palace   dance   wince   trance

Can you say your own sentences using some of the words on these pages?

What other words do you know that are spelled in these ways?

/e/	-ea

head   ready   feather   pleasant   instead

Common exception words

Mr   Mrs   through   eye   could   water

We may say some words differently because of our accent.

Talk about the story

Answer the questions:

1 Where did Gemma eat breakfast and dinner?

2 What kind of things did Gemma and her dad like to look for in the city?

3 Why did Gemma think her dance teacher might be able to tell her more about The Dance Palace?

4 How did Gemma bring her own house to life?

5 What is your favourite kind of music to dance to?

6 If you had a house like Gemma's, what special features would you give it?

Can you retell the story in your own words?